A MUSICAL COLLECTION FROM
CIRQUE DU SOLEIL®

Alfred Publishing Co., Inc.
16320 Roscoe Blvd., Suite 100
P.O. Box 10003
Van Nuys, CA 91410-0003
alfred.com

ISBN-10: 0-7390-4786-8
ISBN-13: 978-0-7390-4786-6

Photos: Al Seib, Camirand, Richard Termine Costumes: Dominique Lemieux © 2003, 2007, Cirque du Soleil Inc.

Contents

PAGEANT
(from "KÀ")

Music by
RENÉ DUPÉRÉ

10

O
(from "O")

Music by
BENOIT JUTRAS

KUNYA SOBÉ

(from "Mystère Live")

Music by
RENÉ DUPÉRÉ

Moderately ♩ = 96

13

Kunya Sobé - 6 - 2
28180

14

ya So - bé____ ma - ni - é - vo.___

Yéké - sou-la___ mo-dié vo, yéké - sou-la___ sé - bo dié.

Yéké - sou - la___ mo-dié vo, yéké - sou-la___ sé - vié.

Yéké - sou - la___ mo-dié vo, yéké - sou-la___ sé - bo dié no.

Yéké - sou-la__ mo-dié vo, yéké - sou-la__ sé - vié.__

Kunya Sobé - 6 - 4
28180

IF I COULD REACH YOUR HEART

(from "KÀ")

Lyrics by
ELLA

Music by
RENÉ DUPÉRÉ

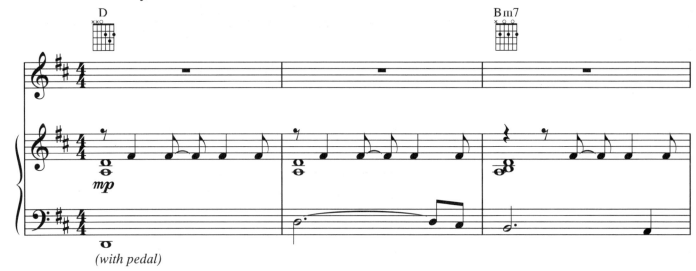

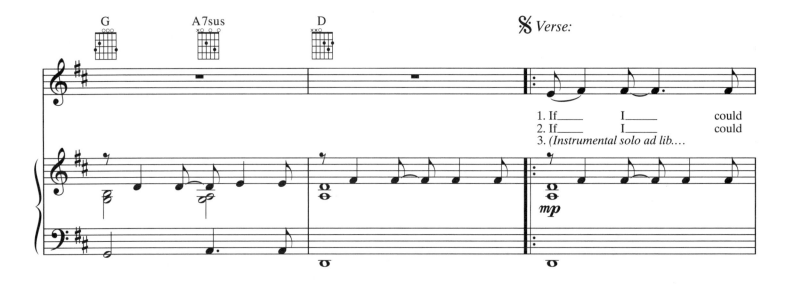

1. If____ I____ could
2. If____ I____ could
3. (Instrumental solo ad lib....

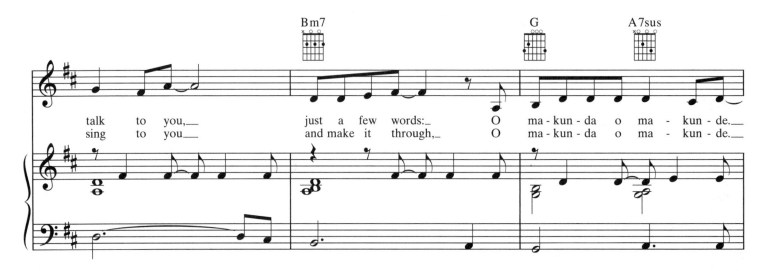

talk to you,____ just a few words:____ O ma-kun-da o ma-kun-de.____
sing to you____ and make it through,____ O ma-kun-da o ma-kun-de.____

If I Could Reach Your Heart - 4 - 1
28180

LOVE DANCE
(from "KÀ")

Music by
RENÉ DUPÉRÉ

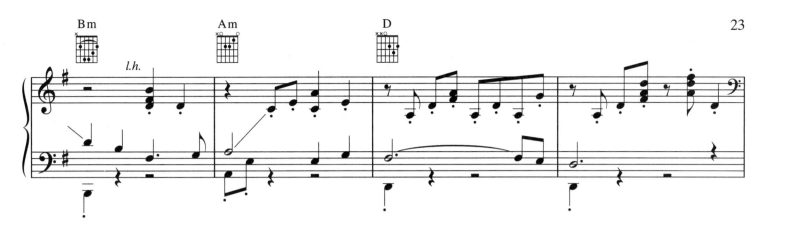

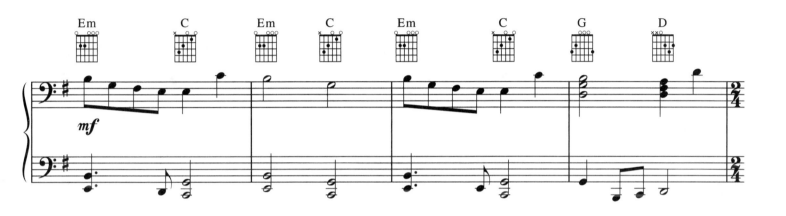

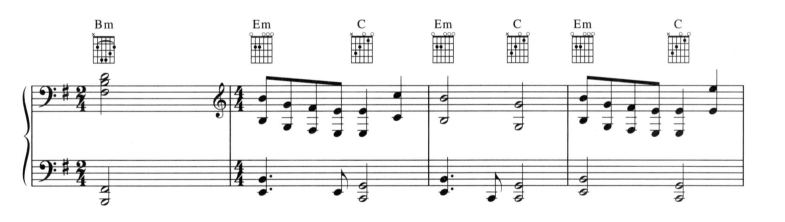

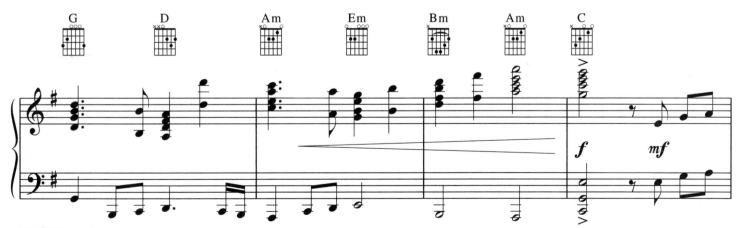

Love Dance - 4 - 2
28180

24

QUERER
(from "Alegría")

Lyrics by
MANUEL TADROS

Music by
RENÉ DUPÉRÉ

28

Gm   Gm7 C7   Fmaj7 B♭maj7 E7sus A7

lar,   des - cu-brir la be - lle - - za del mar.   Que -

Dm   A7sus Dm   A7

rer,   y po - der com-par - tir   nues - tra sed de vi -

Dm   F#dim7 Gm   B♭/F Em7(♭5) A7

vir.   El re - ga - lo que nos da el a-mor,   es la

1.
Dm   A7sus   2. Dm   Dm/C   D.S. %

vi - da.   vi - da.

ALEGRÍA
(from "Alegría")

Lyrics by
FRANCO DRAGONE,
MANUEL TADROS and
CLAUDE AMESSE

Music by
RENÉ DUPÉRÉ

Moderately slow ♩ = 88

(with pedal)

32

ren.
treme.
Co-me la ra - bia___ di a mar,   a-le-
There is a love in___ me rag - ing,   a-le-

grí - a,___   co-me un as - sal - to___ di gio -
grí - a,___   a joy-ous, mag - i - cal feel -

1.2.
ia.
ing.   *(Instrumental solo)*

2.3. A-le -

dad. There is a love in____ me rag - ing, a - le -

grí - a,____ a joy-ous, mag - i - cal feel - ing.

decresc.

mp

(Instrumental solo)

Repeat ad lib. and fade

Verse 4:
Alegría, como la luz de la vida, alegría.
Como un payaso que grita, alegría.
Del estupendo grito,
De la tristeza loca serena.
Como la rabia de amar, alegría
Como un asalto de felicidad.

TRIANGLE TANGO

(from "Corteo")

Music by
PHILIPPE LEDUC

38

Ya   ya da ya da da   ya da   ya ya.   Ya   ya da da da da   ya da   ya da.

QUIDAM
(from "Quidam")

Lyrics by
JIM CORCORAN

Music by
BENOIT JUTRAS

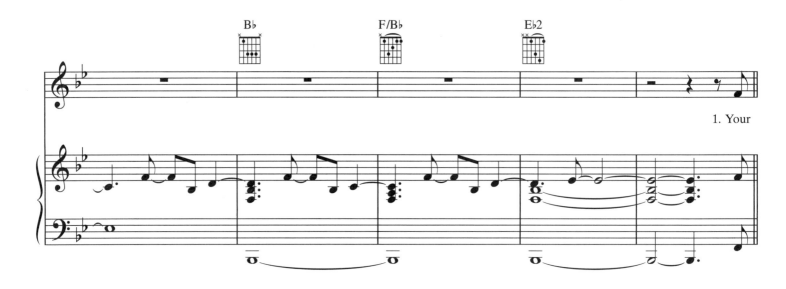

1. Your

Verse 1:

world is yours,___ not mine,___ Qui - dam.___ Your dreams are yours._____ You

Quidam - 8 - 1
28180

B♭(9) F/B♭ E♭9
may have touched the stars, but they weren't moved.
B♭(9) F/B♭
And if you reach for me, I may not
Gm E♭ B♭(9) F/B♭
choose to hold your hand. I might smile, or I might turn a -
E♭9 D7/F♯ Gm
way. An or - di - nar - y man, Qui - dam. I'm

44

46

Chorus:

OMBRA
(from "Dralion")

Lyrics by
HÉLÈNE DORION

Music by
VIOLAINE CORRADI

Moderately, flowing latin feel (♩ = 132)

52

54

56

(Instrumental fills)

Interlude:

58

La___ gio - ia___ ci ri - ve - la - no. Co - me___ si

dà il___ fio - re al so - le. Il tem - po

sem - pre___ vol - ge - ra___ È il___ nos - tro

(Spoken:) Des jours fragiles... ...et nuits sans défense,... ...la roue tournero.

viag - gio.___

LET ME FALL
(from "Quidam")

Lyrics by
JIM CORCORAN

Music by
BENOIT JUTRAS

Very slowly, with feeling (♩ = 66)

(with pedal)

Let me

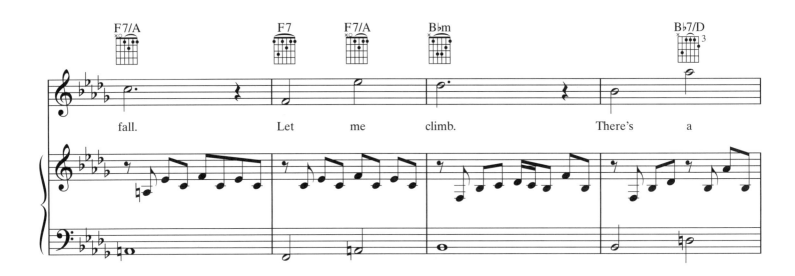

fall.   Let   me   climb.   There's   a

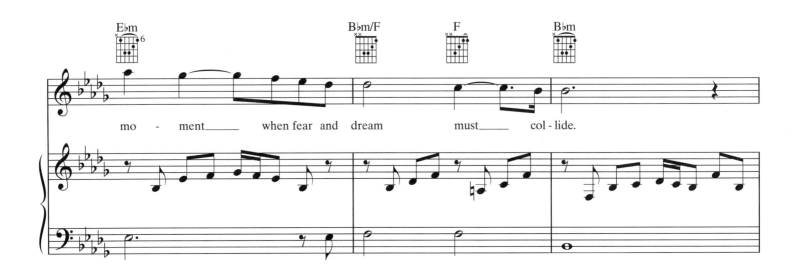

mo - ment   when fear and dream   must   col - lide.

Let Me Fall - 6 - 1
28180

ALONE
(from "DELIRIUM")

Lyrics by
ROBBIE DILLON and
MANUEL TADROS

Music by
RENÉ DUPÉRÉ

TIME FLIES
(from "DELIRIUM")

Lyrics by
ROBBIE DILLON

Music by
BENOIT JUTRAS and
FRANCIS COLLARD

Moderately fast dance feel ♩ = 128

Verse 1:
Bm

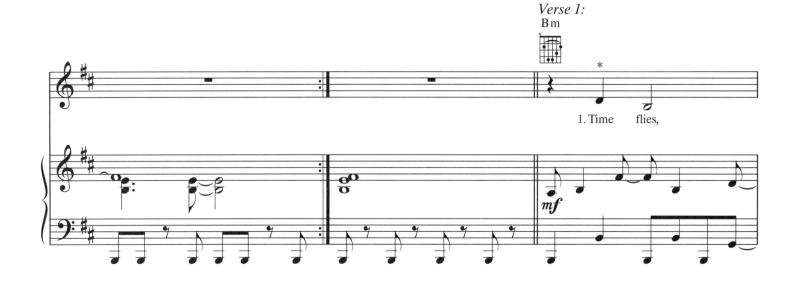

1. Time flies,

leav-ing be-hind__ fad-ed smiles_ and a pho-to-graph._

*All vocals written at pitch.

Time Flies - 8 - 1
28180

72

Time Flies - 8 - 3
28180

MIO BELLO BELLO AMORE
(from "Zumanity: Another Side of Cirque du Soleil")

Lyrics by
ANNA LIANI

Music by
SIMON CARPENTIER

82

NOSTALGIE
(from "O")

Music by
BENOIT JUTRAS

LIAMA
(from "La Nouba")

Music by
BENOIT JUTRAS

Slowly ♩ = 72

(with pedal)

1. Mi -

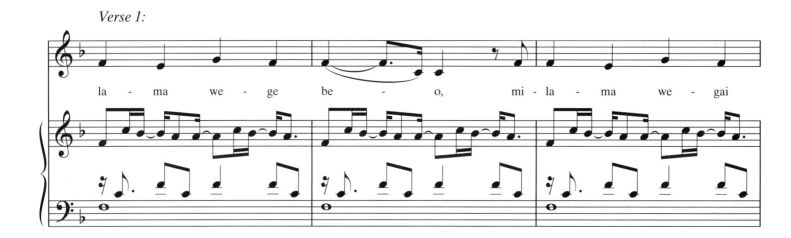

Verse 1:

la - ma we - ge be - o, mi - la - ma we - gai

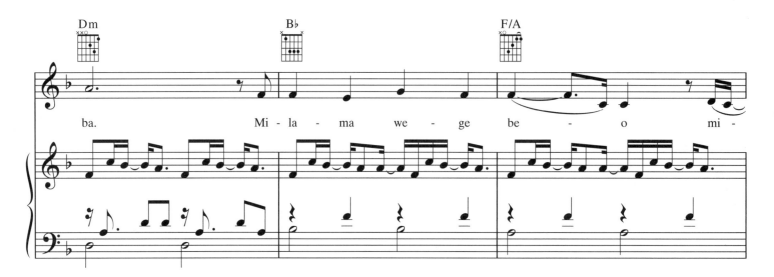

ba. Mi - la - ma we - ge be - o mi -

92

POKINOÏ

(from "Saltimbanco")

Music by
RENÉ DUPÉRÉ

Chorus:

Po - ki - noï,_____

Po - ki - noï._____

Accordion solo:

1. 2.

du brach ti - vo.
du brach ti - vo.

Po - ki - noï.

Repeat and fade

KUMBALAWÉ
(from "Saltimbanco")

Music by
RENÉ DUPÉRÉ

GAMELAN
(from "O")

Music by
BENOIT JUTRAS

Misterioso (♩ = 120)

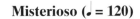

Ma - sai - yah yon - ta - la. Ma - sai - yah yon - ta - la.

(optional, with vocal)

Ma - sai - yah yon - ta - la. Ma - sai - yah yon - ta - la.

Ma - sai - yah yon - ta - la. Ma - sai - yah yon - ta - la.

mp

Gamelan - 9 - 1
28180

Ma - sai - yah   yon - ta - la.   Ma - sai - yah   yon - ta - la

beh.

So - be -

E♭m   N.C.
(modal outline, Dorian in nature.)

yah ton-yah ko-ton-ya leh.___ So-be - yah so-beh a - leh.___ Ko-ba-

108

Gamelan - 9 - 4
28180

112

L'INNOCENT
(from "KOOZA")

Music by
JEAN-FRANÇOIS CÔTÉ

L'innocent - 6 - 1
28180

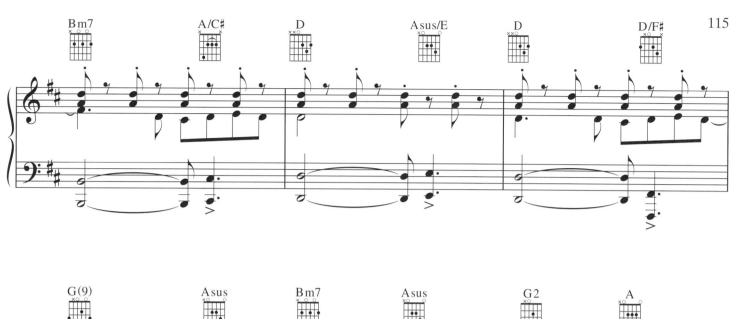

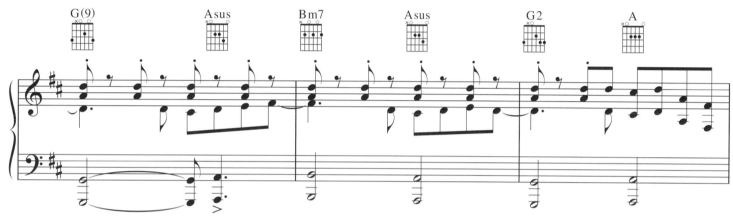

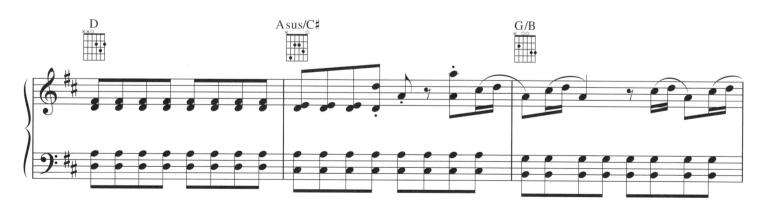

116

*Lyrics represent non-translating syllables.

L'innocent - 6 - 3
28180

Original feel

N.C.

off do   a bre eh   a bre eh   bea   de.

THE MUSIC OF
CIRQUE DU SOLEIL®

«O™»

MYSTÈRE™ LIVE

SALTIMBANCO™

DRALION™

LE BEST OF

ALEGRÍA™

QUIDAM™

LA NOUBA™

VAREKAI™

CORTEO™

ZUMANITY™

SOLARIUM-DELIRIUM
REMIX

KÀ™

DELIRIUM

AVAILABLE
FALL 2007

KOOZA™

NOW AVAILABLE ON CD!

CIRQUEDUSOLEIL.COM

Photo: Al Seib Costume: Dominique Lemieux © 2004 Cirque du Soleil Inc.